Teaching Anger Management and Problem-solving Skills

www.luckyduck.co.uk

Teaching Anger Management and Problem-solving Skills

Brian Marris and Tina Rae

P·C·P
Paul Chapman
Publishing

Paul Chapman Publishing
A SAGE Publications Company
1 Oliver's Yard
55 City Road
London EC1Y 1SP

SAGE Publications Inc.
2455 Teller Road
Thousand Oaks, California 91320

SAGE Publications India Pvt Ltd
B-42, Panchsheel Enclave
Post Box 4109
New Delhi 110 017

www.luckyduck.co.uk

Commissioning Editor: George Robinson
Editorial Team: Wendy Ogden, Sarah Lynch, Mel Maines
Designer: Jess Wright

A catalogue record for this book is available from the British Library
Library of Congress Control Number 2006900704

ISBN 10 1-4129-1935-5

ISBN 13 978-1-4129-1935-7

Printed on paper from sustainable resources

Printed in Great Britain by The Cromwell Press Ltd, Trowbridge, Wiltshire

Contents

Acknowledgements

The authors would like to thank and acknowledge the support and input from the following colleagues and also the pupils of the Junior PRU: Janine Koeries (Head of Junior PRU) and Alice Weston (Support Assistant).

Thanks to all of the staff at the Hillingdon Tuition centre who gave so much time and support in devising this programme.

A note on gender

Rather than repeat throughout the programme the modern but cumbersome 's/he', we have decided to use both genders equally throughout the range of activities. In no way are we suggesting a stereotype for either gender in any activity. We believe that you can adapt if the example you are given does not correspond to the gender of the child in front of you!

How to use the CD-ROM

The CD-ROM contains PDF files, labelled 'Worksheets.pdf' which consists of worksheets for each lesson in this resource. You will need Acrobat Reader version 3 or higher to view and print these resources.

To photocopy the worksheets directly from this book, set your photocopier to enlarge by 125% and align the edge of the page to be copied against the leading edge of the copier glass (usually indicated by an arrow).

Introduction and Rationale

The Government's recent agenda for inclusion in schools and the focus on preventing and reducing exclusions has further raised awareness as to the specific needs of students with social, emotional and behavioural difficulties. Many mainstream schools have consequently had to rethink how these students are both supported and managed within this context. Under the Excellence in Cities Initiative schools have been able to further access student referral units and learning support units alongside setting up on-site units and introducing and implementing Pastoral Support Plans (PSPs).

A plethora of programmes has also been developed with the aim of providing students with opportunities to develop the social, emotional and behavioural skills that they need in order to both access the curriculum and to succeed socially in the mainstream classroom context. Many of these programmes involve collaboration between SENCOs and specialist facilitators, including learning mentors and outside support agencies such as educational psychologists, mental health professionals and education social workers. The success of these programmes is usually dependent upon whether or not the whole-school framework and policy for promoting positive behaviour and emotional literacy is in place and truly effective. Approaches based on cognitive behavioural therapy and solution-focused psychology generally appear to be effective in ensuring the inclusion of most at risk students. However, there remains a group of harder to reach pupils who may well become permanently excluded from school and are consequently required to attend a Pupil Referral Unit (PRU) prior to being either reintegrated into the mainstream context or accessing special provision. It is with this group of students in mind that the Daniel's Letters programme has been developed in order to support children aged 9–12 who have been permanently excluded from their schools.

Staff at the PRU were keen to develop an emotionally literate approach and context in which to successfully engage with and promote change within the students. They were also keen to develop a programme of support which would build upon the good practice found in many mainstream schools. Most importantly, it was felt necessary to develop a programme which would specifically address the concerns and needs of younger students who had been permanently excluded from school. A central aim was to de-mystify the whole process of exclusion and reintegration and to ensure that they would be provided with the opportunity to develop the kinds of skills that they might well need in order to transfer successfully back into the mainstream context.

Mental health issues and the concept of emotional literacy

It is essential to highlight the fact that the students for whom this programme was initially developed had all encountered difficult situations in the past and problems in a range of both school and social contexts. Such negative experiences, alongside frequent rejections by significant adults, had often led to aggressive or withdrawn behaviours and for many of the children targeted, a degree of depression. In the light of these experiences, many of these children could be described as not being particularly 'mentally healthy'.

A study by the Mental Health Foundation (*The Big Picture*, February 1999) focused upon the promotion of children and young people's mental health. This report defined the mentally healthy as those with the ability to:

- develop psychologically, emotionally, creatively, intellectually and spiritually

- initiate, develop and sustain mutually satisfying personal relationships

- use and enjoy solitude

- become aware of others and empathise with them

- play and learn

- develop a sense of right and wrong

- face problems and setbacks and learn from them in ways appropriate for the child's age.

This report also identifies the fact that since the 1940s the number of children experiencing mental ill health has increased to one in five. The authors also suggest that these mental health problems will continue to increase unless there is a clear and holistic programme implemented to develop the emotional and mental health of our children. In recent years the DfES have piloted the SEBS curriculum (Social, Emotional and Behavioural Skills curriculum) within primary schools in 25 LEAs in order to go some way towards meeting such a goal. This programme of support aims to address the emotional, social and behavioural needs that many children may exhibit at some point in their school careers. It also aims to promote an emotionally literate and mentally healthy school context and environment in which teachers and pupils can successfully learn and work together. This is entirely laudable. However, for some children, as stated earlier, there will be a need to provide something in addition to this programme of support in order to ensure that they can develop the kinds of skills they need in order to remain successfully within the mainstream context.

Solution-focused approach

In order to facilitate the growth of students' ability to self-reflect, self-monitor and set appropriate targets, this programme adopts a solution-focused approach. This powerful approach is described by Rhodes and Ajmal (1995) as being a significant and incredibly useful tool in supporting students through the process of change as they state:

> In supporting students ... in their wish to change what is happening, we have found no model of approaching behaviour difficulties more useful and flexible than solution-focused thinking. (Page 55.)

This appears to be because this kind of process encourages students to formulate a new and more positive story for themselves, one in which their skills, strengths and resources can be both identified and reinforced. Consequently, from the first session onwards, the students are encouraged to consider the kinds of resources and strategies that they would need in order to be more effective and to begin to describe and recognise these within themselves from the outset.

Two types of learning

Dealing with emotions in terms of relating to oneself and to others is a complex issue. People generally need both education and skill-based learning in order to gain the skills that they need in order to be effective both socially, emotionally and academically. As Margot Sunderland and Philip Engleheart (1993) suggest, 'It is a mockery to say that a person's emotional life takes care of itself. It clearly does not.' (Page 2.) Consequently, this programme aims to provide this kind of skill-based learning which focuses specifically on teaching students the kinds of self-management and emotional control skills that they will need in order to become reintegrated successfully back into the mainstream context.

Two types of learning have been identified by psychologists: cognitive learning (which involves absorbing new data and gaining insights into existing frameworks of association) and emotional learning. It is the emotional learning which appears to involve engaging the part of the brain where our emotional signature is stored. This tends to demand or involve new ways of thinking. Cognitive learning appears to be more clear cut and straightforward but emotional learning is more complex and difficult. It is harder for an individual to accept the fact that they may need to improve their ability to control their temper or manage their angry feelings than it is to engage them in learning a new cognitive skills. As Dann (2001) suggests the prospect of needing to develop greater emotional intelligence is likely to generate some resistance to change. It is not easy to accept the fact that you need to make such changes and, consequently, this has been taken into account when planning Daniel's Letters. The programme focuses throughout on promoting, fostering and motivating students to effect change by solution-focused processes. They are encouraged to continually self-reflect, self-monitor and set realistic and achievable targets and goals. This is a continual and cyclical process involving a series of key questions as follows:

- What are my key skills?

- What goes well and why?

- What doesn't go well and why?

- How can I change unhelpful patterns of behaviour? (Learning to visualise and choose a new response.)

Objectives of the programme

The Daniel's Letters programme consists of weekly group sessions over a ten week period and these aim to meet the following objectives:

- To encourage students to develop an awareness of their own feelings.

- To enable students to label feelings and to know when they may or may not affect both work and relationships.

- To enable students to further develop personal insight.

- To develop students' self-esteem and self-confidence.

- To enable students to accept and utilise structured, constructive criticism and feedback.

- To encourage students to develop self-control and self-management strategies.

- To encourage students to develop empathy and authenticity.

- To encourage students to take responsibility for their behaviours and actions and to be able to admit to mistakes and errors.

- To enable students to develop flexibility in order to cope more effectively with change and new systems and ways of doing things.

- To encourage students to develop self-motivation, resilience and a positive attitude.

- To help students develop the locus of control, i.e. to encourage them to have internal control.

- To encourage students to learn and make use of alternatives to physical or verbal aggression and to express their feelings and views in a positive and assertive way.

- To encourage facilitators and support staff to adopt a consistent approach in terms of developing students' emotional literacy, social skills and self-esteem.

- To further enable and encourage facilitators to review current policy and practice in terms of managing the emotional, social and behavioural needs of students in their care and to further develop the most appropriate reintegration programmes.

The extent to which these objectives are met is perhaps the best indicator as to the success or otherwise of this programme.

The structure of the programme

The programme is divided into ten sessions. Overall, the sessions aim to teach and reinforce the key skills of emotional literacy as follows:

- awareness of feelings

- personal insight

- self-assurance

- self-regulation

- authenticity

- accountability

- flexibility

- self-motivation.

Each session provides a complete lesson.

Structure of the sessions

Each of the sessions is structured in a similar way as follows:

Warm-up activity

The facilitator can clarify the main aims of the session by recording these on a white board and talking briefly through each point with the students at the start of the group session. It may also be helpful to highlight the structure of the session, for example, Warm-up activity, Daniel's Letter's questions, Worksheet and so on, so that students get used to the format and are aware of what can be expected of them at each stage in the session. The facilitator can then introduce the warm-up games activity. This activity is intended to break down any barriers and provide a positive climate in which to introduce the topic to be covered in the session. The warm-up activities generally take place within the Circle Time framework and it will be necessary to ensure that adequate seating arrangements are made so that each student can have a chair within the circle and any relevant equipment is gathered for the particular game prior to the start of the session. During Session 1 the students initially agree group rules and it is important that adequate time is allocated so as to ensure ownership of these rules and that each student adheres to these in subsequent sessions. It may be helpful to reinforce group rules prior to clarifying the aims or content of each subsequent session. They also focus specifically on promoting cooperation, self-esteem and empathy.

Daniel's Letters

The script for Daniel's Letters is then read out by the facilitator prior to considering a series of questions around the issues identified. In these letters Daniel describes the ways in which he copes with the new context he finds himself in. As he details how he copes with stress, angry feelings, managing his behaviour and that of others, the students are able to identify with his feelings, thoughts and behaviours. It is hoped that by raising the issues and emotions around the exclusion process in this way that students can then be provided with a safe forum in which to consider their own feelings and thoughts and also to further reflect upon their own future hopes and dreams and the skills they may need to develop in order to achieve these. Providing Daniel as an example is not intended to suggest that girls do not get excluded or are not at risk of exclusion from school. We chose to use a male protagonist simply because many more boys than girls are excluded and students of both sexes at this stage in their development tend to have fewer difficulties in identifying with and relating to one and another.

Questions for discussion

The students are presented with a series of questions and these can be recorded prior to the start of the session by the facilitator utilising the white board as appropriate. One of the students may wish to act as a scribe to record contributions or, alternatively, the facilitator may wish to continue to take on this role, particularly if students are not literate or have difficulties in this area. The questions generally focus on the contents of Daniel's letters and the idea again is to encourage and generate discussion and to enable students to develop their own ideas and strategies for moving themselves forward and changing their own behaviours, thoughts and feelings.

Worksheet activity

The facilitator can introduce the sheets, which aim to both clarify and reinforce a specific topic introduced within the session. The sheets generally require minimal amounts of recording such as drawing, writing or discussing. It may be helpful for students to have made up individual folders or files in which to present these sheets. These can be made up prior to the start of the course or during Session 1. However, it is advisable to allocate some additional time to this process as it can be time consuming, particularly if students are keen on presenting their work well.

It will be necessary to take note of students whose recording skills are under-developed as they will possibly require additional peer or adult support during some of the activities. However, it is anticipated that the facilitator would be skilled in differentiation and able to ensure that all students have access to the session content regardless of level of ability. Setting up paired working or support systems is a useful idea. Once again, these activities aim to promote the development of personal skills and particularly foster students' ability to cooperate and work effectively as a member of a group.

Plenary

This part of the session enables the students to feedback their ideas and responses from the activity sheets and their view on the contents of the session as whole. It may be helpful for the facilitator to briefly summarise the main concepts covered and to record students' responses on the flip chart or white board. This will encourage the highlighting of experiences that may be common to the majority of the students. It can also help to reinforce any useful, or not so useful, strategies or techniques covered within the session. It can provide students with an opportunity to highlight any of their own difficulties or concerns and to jointly problem-solve the best ways of moving themselves forwards.

Using the programme – notes for facilitators

Although this programme has been developed within the context of a PRU and subsequently used with small groups, it would be feasible to adapt resources as appropriate for larger groups of students. However, it should be stressed that as the main focus in this programme is on supporting pupils aged 9-12 to reintegrate them back into mainstream schools and to develop the kinds of skills they need in order to do this effectively, it may be most appropriate to use this resource as originally intended. We would suggest, that groups of 8-10 students supported by 2-3 adults seem to benefit most from this type of approach. A smaller, more nurturing and less judgemental climate can then be set to support each other in the process of change. The central idea here is that of attempting to engage such students by recognising and validating their experiences and encouraging them to empathise with others who are experiencing the same difficulties. This will not be the 'life story' of all the children who undertake some of the activities unless this programme is actually delivered within the context of a Junior PRU with students who have been permanently excluded from mainstream school.

When trialling this programme for the first time, it was possible to allocate the classroom teacher, the LSA and the Educational Psychologist to the target group in order to deliver each of the sessions. These individuals were also able to provide ongoing tutorial and 1:1 mentoring support for individual students and their parents, alongside delivering the programme. However, it does not necessarily follow that the same arrangement should, or could, be made in other contexts.

Looking forward

Once the programme has been completed (generally as part of a comprehensive and well thought out re-integration package), it is anticipated that the majority of the students will be reintegrated into the mainstream context. The formats for the Welcome Pack, which are found in the appendix, perhaps indicate the extent to which we feel that schools should be aiming to include students who will have been targeted in such groups. It will obviously be helpful to provide ongoing support and to ensure that the system for reintegration is clarified at the outset. This may well need to involve staff from the PRU supporting the student for the first few weeks in the mainstream context and appropriate staff in the mainstream context visiting the PRU in order to not only get to know the student but also to familiarise themselves with the kind of emotional and social skills curriculum that the child has had access to. However this is arranged, it is important to highlight the fact that support will need to be relatively intense initially and then reduced gradually as progress in made, confidence is further built and the skills are evidently transferred into this new context.

It is hoped that this programme is able to build upon current good practice in both mainstream schools and PRUs and positive initiatives for students with social, emotional and behavioural difficulties. Its basis in solution-focused processes, interactionism and emotional well-being initiatives will hopefully provide facilitators with a dynamic and successful way forward in terms of ensuring the reintegration of some of our most vulnerable children.

Case Study

Our experiences of using the material:

Ben came to the Pupil Referral Unit (PRU) on a dual role placement which meant that he spent one term initially in the PRU and maintained his place in his mainstream primary school. He had not been permanently excluded from school but had a fixed term exclusion for this period of time on the agreement that he would attend the PRU and participate in the course on offer. As part of his programme he was required to participate in the Daniel's Letters programme which was actually developed and trialled with Ben's peer group. In his mainstream classroom context he'd been regarded as a bully and many teachers here described him as being a troublemaker. He subsequently received six fixed term exclusions prior to this longer exclusion due to inappropriate and violent behaviour towards others. However, he felt that his teachers had very often set up situations in order to wind him up and cause him to fail.

During initial discussions with staff at the PRU, Ben's parents (mum and stepfather) both decided and stated that they wanted him to return to a mainstream school and become 'normal' and 'less angry'. Although Ben did initially present as a very angry and quite distressed little boy he soon settled down in the PRU and it became quickly very apparent that he relished positive adult attention and interaction. This was something that he actually sought out.

During the first session, 'Being excluded', Ben found it quite difficult to participate in the Circle Time context. He had clearly not been used to participating in such activities. However, with the facilitators support Ben was able to identify how it was possible to actually have a new start and to come from a difficult situation into a new and a less stressful one. Ben said that he would advise Daniel to be very honest about the reasons for his exclusion, e.g. fighting and abusing the teacher, as he felt that being honest was a 'good thing'.

Ben responded positively to the second session. He was able to put his triggers to anger in the most common, least common order. However, in a subsequent session (Session 3) Ben found it difficult to maintain his anger diary and was rather reluctant to record his feelings on each day of the week as required. At this stage it became apparent that most of his anger was centred around two individuals within his new peer group whom he perceived to be slightly aggressive and bullying towards him. He was reluctant to discuss his feelings with staff in the PRU as he was beginning to feel quite vulnerable and not really in control of his own situation.

In Session 4 Daniel loses his temper and has an extremely bad end to his week at the PRU. Ben was able to empathise with this in that he had had a couple of arguments in the playground over football and these had led to some aggressive responses. However, he was, with practising, able to talk through the problems with his class teacher and showed that he was now more able to reflect on his behaviours and their outcomes. He was also able to accept the fact that we all make mistakes. It's how we remedy this that is important.

During Session 6, 'Coping with loss and taking time out', Ben began to reveal the extent to which he could actually empathise with others in a really meaningful way. He began to articulate how losing his dad had upset him when he was a little boy (approximately five or six years old) and how he was aware that his granny and his mum had both been affected by his dad's death. It was significant and of real interest to the facilitators that Ben, along with all the six children in this group, had experienced a significant loss or bereavement in his early years. In this session, the introduction of the time out strategy for difficult moments was something that Ben decided that he could adopt and make use of both now and in the future. Knowing he could have the option of withdrawing himself from difficult situations in this way helped him to feel less stressed and more in control. However, during Session 7, it did become apparent that Ben found it difficult to talk about problems and situations that caused him concern with members of his peer group. This activity required students to jointly problem-solve and the whole process was difficult for Ben who tended to put down the other child in his pair, perhaps mainly due to his own fragile self-esteem.

The facilitators had to intervene at this stage and it quickly became apparent that Ben still felt very vulnerable and lacking in confidence when interacting with his peers. However, he was able to make use of this problem-solving framework with the adult to take the lead and offer him the kind of support that was unconditional and positive and did not demand of him that he find the solutions solely on his own.

Ben did not attend for Session 8 as he was sick but it was possible to discuss the contents of the session with him on his return to the PRU. As most of the students in the group found it difficult initially to make use of 'I' statements, additional time was given in order to provide them with opportunities to role play a variety of different problem situations, making use of 'I' statements in order to respond in a more positive and assertive way to difficult situations. Initially, Ben acted out a little sample; rather than saying to another child, 'I want you to stop trying to take my mobile phone,' he said, 'I'll kick your head in if you do that again.' He insisted that he was still making an 'I' statement which, on one level, is absolutely correct. However, after he'd got over the initial embarrassment of having to engage in role-play, he was able to make use of more appropriate 'I' statements and did realise that this could be a positive strategy for him to use in future situations of conflict and difficulty.

In the final session, Ben was able to identify many strategies that he had learnt during the course that he felt would work for him and did work for him currently. He was particularly keen to mention the use of time out, deep breathing strategies and the stepped approach to problem-solving. Ben was also able to identify specific targets for himself which included moving away from people who were aggressive towards him, ignoring comments about his mum and being kind and listening to both his peers and teachers. It was interesting that when asked what he could do to help himself, Ben suggested that he could try and 'keep happy' because when he was happy he knew he wouldn't get angry with other people. This was very positive as Ben was clearly beginning to be able to recognise and make use of strategies that worked for him.

By the time the course had been completed, Ben's ability to analyse his behaviours and understand the consequences of behaviours had increased dramatically as had his level of empathy and locus of control. Ben had clearly achieved some success within this smaller group context and as he neared the end of the course, he displayed mixed emotions. This was consistent with Daniel in his letters to group.

Ben obviously wanted to return to school but was extremely fearful as to whether or not he could really succeed. In order to support him in this, the staff involved organised a reintegration package for him which included the following:

- LSA support for his class to target the rest of the class, i.e. not Ben.

- A mentor was identified.

- A circle of friends was set up by PRU staff and reinforced by additional support sessions in the second term.

- Strategies regarding behaviour management and ideas and resources used in this programme were given to his teacher when he returned to mainstream school.

- A home/school link system was set up by the PRU staff to ensure parental support and participation.

- Mentor to parent link times were set up to ensure home/school links were truly effective.

These strategies were explained to Ben and certainly went some way to reassure him on his transfer back to mainstream school. He remained in mainstream school until the end of Year 6 and then successfully transferred to high school. It seems that his relationship with his parents improved to some extent and he is currently described as a child who can cope in mainstream by staff. It seems that there are fewer incidences of Ben responding aggressively to others' aggression and more occasions when he is able to utilise the strategies taught within the context of the PRU. Although Ben is not described as a 'perfect' or 'model pupil', he is described as a child who can and will be able to achieve in the mainstream setting.

This is a real success story which is due, in the main, to the commitment, expertise and inclusive approaches of all the staff involved and also to Ben's capacity to change and relearn behaviours and attitudes. Although the course cannot be said to have provided Ben with all the answers and all the strategies that he might need, we did feel that to some extent it did go some way towards providing him with an initial opportunity to review his behaviour and understand and accept the fact that he could and would be able to change. It also gave him the opportunity to further understand the perspectives of others, particularly adults who work with him and to realise that, like him, they could also feel anger, humiliation and fear. What was most important was that they should be able to both acknowledge and cope with such difficult and complex emotions.

References

Boulger, E. (2002) *Building on Social Skills*, Staffordshire, Nasen.

Casey, J. (2002) *Getting it Right: A Behaviour Curriculum*, Bristol, Lucky Duck Publishing.

Dann, J. (2001) *Emotional Intelligence in a Week*, Oxford, Hodder & Stroughton

De Shazar, S. (1988) *Clues: Investigating Solutions in Brief Therapy*, New York, Norton.

Elias, M. J. & Clabby, J. (1992) *Building Social and Emotional Development in Deaf Children,* The PATH Programme, Seattle, University of California Press.

Faupel, A., Herrick, E. & Sharp, P. (1998) *Solution Talk: Hosting Therapeutic Conversations*, New York, Norton.

Goleman, E. (1995) *Emotional Intelligence – Why it can matter more than IQ,* London, Bloomsbury.

Gourley, P. (1999) *Teaching Self -control in the Classroom – a Cognitive Behavioural Approach*, Bristol, Lucky Duck Publishing.

Greenberg, M.T. & Kushche, C.A. (1993) *Promoting Social and Emotional Development in Deaf Children*, The PATH Programme, Seattle, University of California Press.

Johnson, P. & Rae, T. (1999) *Crucial Skills – An Anger Management and Problem Solving Teaching Programme for High School Students*, Bristol, Lucky Duck Publishing.

Rae, T. (1998) *Dealing with Feeling*, Bristol, Lucky Duck Publishing.

Rae, T. (2000) *Confidence, Assertiveness, Self Esteem – A Series of Twelve Sessions for Secondary School Students*, Bristol, Lucky Duck Publishing.

Rae, T. (2001) *Strictly Stress – Effective Stress Management for High School Students*, Bristol, Lucky Duck Publishing.

Rae, T. (2004) *Dealing With More Feelings*, Bristol, Lucky Duck Publishing.

Rae, T. & Marris, B. (2004) *Escape From Exclusion*, Bristol, Lucky Duck Publishing.

Rhodes, J. & Ajimal, Y. (1995) *Solution-focused Thinking in Schools,* London, Brief Therapy Publication.

Sheldon, B. (1995) *Cognitive Behavioural Therapy: Research, Practice and Philosophy*, London, Routledge.

Sunderland, M. & Engleheart, P. (1993) *Draw on your Emotions*, Oxford Speechmark.

Wardle, C. & Rae, T. (2002) *School Survival – Helping Students Survive and Succeed in Secondary School*, Bristol, Lucky Duck Publishing.

Warden, E. & Christie, E. (1997) *Teaching Social Behaviour*, London, David Fulton Publishers.

White, M. (1999) *Picture This – Guided Imagery for Circle Time*, Bristol, Lucky Duck Publishing.

Session 1

Being Excluded

Introduction

During the introduction to the session it will be helpful for the facilitator to describe the basic contents of the course and the rationale for students actually participating in the course. It would be helpful to outline reasons why the students have been excluded from school and the purpose of the PRU placement. It will then also be important to formulate group rules prior to starting the first games activity. Setting group rules should lead on from the discussion of the course objectives. It is essential that students have the time to agree and discuss their own set of rules so as to ensure ownership of them and that everyone in the group or class adheres to them in each of the subsequent sessions. These rules may include the following:

- We agree to keep our discussions private to the group and not chat about it with others outside of the group.

- We will all try to make some kind of contribution that is positive and think of ideas in each session.

- We will not put each other down or make fools of each other.

- We will try to work together and respect each other's point of view.

- We will try to look after each other and back each other up.

- No one in our group will be made to say anything if they don't want to.

- We won't use put-downs.

The idea here is to create, from the outset, an empathic and supportive framework in which the students can learn to trust each other and develop their own skills and strategies.

Warm-up activity – 'Getting to Know You'

This first warm up activity is intended to break down any barriers between the students and provide a relaxed ethos to the group from the outset. Students can be seated as for Circle Time and obviously the rules agreed at the start of the session will apply in this context also. The first game that they'll be introduced to is just a 'getting to know you' game. Each student will be asked to hold a discussion for two minutes with the person next to them, (sitting on their left-hand side) in order to find out three things that they have in common. These will then be fed back to the group as a whole. Students can feedback for each other or one student may feedback for each pair.

Daniel's Letters

In his first letter Daniel introduces himself as a 9½ year old boy who has been permanently excluded from school. He is about to start at the local PRU and is rather worried and anxious about this. Daniel describes how he feels labelled by his teachers in his previous school and how his parents are both very anxious and angry with him for the behaviours that he has shown in that context. Daniel is feeling very much out of control and rather depressed at this stage.

The facilitator reads the letters as follows:

Dear Friend,

I've heard you are having trouble in school and might be suspended or have been suspended. I though I'd write to you to tell you my story. My name is Daniel and I am 9½ years old. I used to go to Willow Lane Primary School but yesterday was my last day – they finally kicked me out. Things have been getting bad for quite a while. I knew the teachers didn't like me any more because they kept putting me in detention all the time and excluding me from playtimes. They said it was all my fault because I was rude and kept fighting other people and getting angry all the time. I don't think that's true though I did get quite angry with lots of people, especially the other boys in my class but it wasn't always my fault. In the end, just because I was bad sometimes, the teachers just said I was bad all the time and it was always me when it wasn't. That made me even more angry. So, I just started to lie and say it wasn't me at all even if I knew it was. I knew they would blame me anyway. Then I would get excluded for good. I had three exclusions before but they were all for a few days and that was mainly because I swore at the teacher and punched the deputy headteacher in the leg because she was trying to pull me away from another kid who had just thumped me on the nose. Anyway, I got caught smoking in the toilets and they said I was forcing someone else to smoke with me but I wasn't. Ben wanted a cigarette as well. They did a big report to the Governors and they said that they had never come across anyone quite so insolent as me. I'm not really sure what insolent means but my mum just said it's really rude. Anyway, no one is happy with me that's for sure. My mum's not talking to me and on Monday morning I have got to go and visit this Pupil Referral Unit. That is where they send all the bad people like me or the ones that they can't keep in school because they just don't behave and teachers hate them. Deep down though I am a bit scared about going because I don't think I am all that bad even though I am a bit bad sometimes. I can be all right if I am in a good mood, if people don't make me feel fed up and show me up in class and that.

My dad's furious about it. He said that's it, my life's ruined now because I will always have this record and everyone will always think I am a bad person. He said going to a PRU is a bit like being put into a prison. You are there with all the other bad people and you just become worse because you are learning their tricks. In fact, he said it is a lot like prison so if I am honest; I am not looking forward to it at all. I don't know what to expect. Headteacher said that there will be, like, six people in my class and there will be two teachers in there: one a real teacher and one that helps you with things when you get upset. What will the other kids be like? That's what I am worried about because if they are really bad then how am I going to get to stay there because I will just end up losing my temper and fighting with them as well? I don't know what it is that makes me feel so angry. Sometimes it's just stupid things, silly things, little things, but at the moment I don't feel angry, I just feel really fed up. I don't think it was fair that I was excluded just for smoking. I know there were other things building up to it but I didn't make anyone's nose bleed or anything. I just think the school just got really fed up with me. My mum says she doesn't blame them really because she says I am a pain in the neck. What I am really feeling is just a bit scared I think but I can't tell anyone else that. What is it going to be like? Do you think I will be all right going there? They said it's only for about 15 weeks before they can get me back into another school but how can they guarantee me getting back to another school? They can't make anyone take me can they? I don't know what's going to happen. I feel like everything is out of control and it's not funny anymore.

Yours,

Daniel

Questions for discussion

- Why do you think Daniel was excluded from his mainstream school?

- How do you think he feels about it?

- What does his mum seem to think about the situation?

- How do you think he feels about going to the Pupil Referral Unit?

- What advice would you give to him for when he starts his new placement on Monday?

- If you were writing a letter to Daniel, how would you describe a PRU and how would you help him to feel less frightened?

Worksheet activity – 'Excluded For Good - a Quiz' or 'Going to be Excluded - a Quiz'

The first worksheet activity takes the form of a simple questionnaire. The students are asked to consider their own exclusions from school and why and how these occurred. They are also asked to consider what they may need in the future in order to successfully transfer back into a mainstream context, identifying the kinds of skills and strategies they will need to develop whilst at the PRU.

This activity does not require the students to record information on the sheet. This is a purely verbal activity, designed to get the students communicating with each other and sharing their experiences. We would strongly advise the facilitator to present and deliver the activity in this way as asking students to record at this stage may result in some antipathy towards the programme as a whole.

Plenary

In the plenary session the facilitator can ask students to reflect upon the contents of the session and to identify the things that they feel that they have learnt. It may be helpful to promote the notion of solution-focused thinking, i.e. things may have gone wrong for those students in the past but they now have an opportunity to begin to develop their skills by working from their strengths and setting themselves realistic goals for the future. It may be also helpful to reinforce the notion of accountability and the fact that Daniel's key learning experience will now need to be around accepting the fact that he did do things wrong and now needs to begin to change his behaviours.

Excluded For Good - A Quiz

The Exclusion Quiz

Daniel didn't feel good about being excluded. He was angry, upset and worried about going to the Pupil Referral Unit.

Can you remember how you felt? Try to answer the following questions:

Why were you excluded?

What happened?

How did you feel?

How do you feel now?

What was your first day like at the PRU?

What happened?

How did you feel?

If you went back to a mainstream school now, how do you think you would cope?

What help do you think you would need?

Going To Be Excluded – A Quiz

Daniel felt worried that he might be excluded because his behaviour was not good. He felt angry and concerned about what might happen. How would you feel if you were in his shoes?
Try to answer the following questions:

Why might you be excluded?

What has happened?

How did you feel about this?

How do you feel now?

What do you think may happen to you in the future?

What do you want to happen?

Who can help you to cope better now?

How can you help yourself?

Session 2

Focus on Anger

Warm-up activity – 'Wink Murder'

One student is allocated to be murderer by the facilitator prior to the start of the session. This should be done in secret so that the other students do not know who has been chosen. The student then has to wink at members of the group who are sitting in the circle. If they are winked at they have to pretend to die. They can make some elaborate motions with their arms and legs and also some noises if they so wish! The first student to guess correctly who the murderer is then has to leave the room whilst the new murderer is chosen. Once this has happened, the person is allowed back into the room to rejoin the circle. They are then the only person who can guess who the murderer is and the game continues. Once they have correctly guessed, the murderer is the person who has to wait outside whilst the next murderer is chosen.

Daniel's Letters

The facilitator can then read the entry from Daniel's Letters. In this session, Daniel describes his first day at the PRU and how he and his mum met the headteacher. He also describes some of the differences between the PRU and his own school and generally seems to feel quite pleased with the fact that he is in a smaller group and has access to a great deal more support than he did previously. On his first day he does get into a fight at playtime when another child fouls him in the football game. However, he is quite surprised to find that this is only considered to be 'a blip' and that the teacher describes him as actually being quite good for the rest of the day. Daniel doesn't seem to be used to having such positive feedback and thinks that there is something wrong with the teacher.

The facilitator reads the letters as follows:

Dear Friend,

Well today was my first day at the Pupil Referral Unit. I am not sure what I think about it really. It didn't get off to a brilliant start although some of the teachers seemed nice and at least they smiled at you and seemed to listen to you when you spoke to them. First of all, me and my mum had to go into the headteacher's office. He told us what they would expect of me and how this was my chance to really improve my behaviour so that I can get back to mainstream school. He asked me if I wanted to go back to my old school. I said, 'No,' and my mum said, 'No,' as well because she said she thought the teachers had just labelled me and they wouldn't want me back anyway and if I did go back they would just try and make it difficult for me so that I would get into trouble and they would have to exclude me again. My mum also said that she didn't think that the teachers really liked me. I don't think that is really true – I think they did to begin with but when I got bad they didn't. The headteacher asked me why I thought I got bad and I said I didn't know. I think I do know really but I don't want to tell anyone else – why should I? It's not their business.

Anyway, my dad's long gone now. He has been in prison for three months but none of them know that. They don't know at the old school either, it's none of their business as Mum says. She thinks it has affected my behaviour. She said, 'You are affected by it.' I said, 'No, I am not at all,' but there's no arguing with my mum. She always knows she is right when she is right – that's what she says anyway.

I had the speech about what the rules were and what would happen if I broke them and my mum had sign the form to say that they could restrain me if I got totally out of hand. That sounded a bit weird to me. We went down to my new classroom. It looked all right really. It was much smaller than I thought. There were six computers around the edge of the room. Everyone seemed to have their own workstation. I suppose that's so that they can't thump each other – that's what my mum said.

The teacher was nice. She kept smiling and saying how important it was that I made the most of my chance to sort myself out while I was here and the other lady was nice as well. She made me a cup of tea and gave me a biscuit. I don't think a teacher has ever made me a cup of tea before. It's funny that because I drink tea all the time at home but most people think you don't drink it, don't they, if you are a kid. Anyway, it was OK for the first bit. I just had to sit down and play a game on the computer then we all had to do some reading and literacy. It was quite easy to begin with but I think the teacher saw I could do it easily so she gave me something harder which made me a bit angry but I thought I had better just get on with it since it was my first day. Normally I would not have bothered to do it all.

It was at playtime that things got a bit out of hand. They introduced me to all the kids in my class; there are only five others apart from me. One of them is a great big boy, he is a bit fat as well but I suppose he can't help that and then there is a little one and he does nothing but moan all the time and his breath is really bad. Anyway, we were allowed to play football at playtime so we had a kick about and then, of course, someone fouled me. It was the little one, Tommy. He kicked me quite hard so I just lost it. It's just like what happened in the old school, I just got so angry so quickly I couldn't help it. It was like there was an explosion in my head and it all came out at once through my fists and I punched him on the nose. He staggered backwards and fell over and the teacher came running towards me. She looked really shocked, 'On your first day!' she said as if I was some kind of evil person which I suppose I was really. I didn't say anything back I was just too angry to speak then but I knew I had blown it straight off. Anyway, I got my first warning and I had to stay in for the afternoon break and do some cleaning up to make up for it. Of course, she had to tell Mum at the end of the day but it was funny because when she was telling my mum about it she said, 'But it was only a blip and actually he was rather good for the rest of the day and he did the best work in the class.' I though that was a bit funny really – why is she saying nice things about me when I have acted so bad? Something wrong with that teacher, I think.

Yours,

Daniel

Questions for discussion

- How do you think Daniel felt when he first walked into the Pupil Referral Unit?

- What kinds of rules do you think the headteacher will be telling him about?

- What do you think the main differences would be between his mainstream classroom and the PRU classroom?

- How do you think the other kids in the classroom would have felt about him coming in?

- Why did Daniel think the teachers were quite OK to begin with?

- When did things go wrong and why?

- What do you think Daniel could do to help himself manage his anger better? What advice would you give him?

- What do you think Daniel should do on his second day at the PRU? How do you think he should behave?

- Who helps you when you feel angry and how do you help yourself?

- Can you make a list of all your strategies and then think about those that might be useful for Daniel?

Worksheet activity – 'My Time Bombs'

The students are asked to identify their own triggers to anger and to then rank these in order of the most and least common. It may be helpful to allocate some feedback time here so that students can identify and reflect upon any similarities and differences in their experiences.

Plenary

In the Plenary session the facilitator can once again elicit feedback from the students as to how useful or otherwise they found the session. It may also be a good opportunity to reinforce anger management strategies that the students have agreed they could use to date. This may also be helpful in setting specific targets for individual students over the coming weeks and students may also wish to make use of the anger letters introduced in Session 3 in order to monitor their own progress in this area.

My Time Bombs

What causes you to explode? What lights your fuse?

Write down your triggers on the sheet:

STOP & THINK:

Which are the most common triggers?

Place your triggers in order of the most common and least common.

1.

2.

3.

4.

5.

Session 3
Setting Targets

Warm-up activity – 'In the manner of the word'

In this game the facilitator provides one student with one adverb, e.g. happily, angrily, sadly, etc. That student is then asked to mime an action in the manner of the word to the rest of the group who are sitting in the circle as for Circle Time. For example, miming brushing your teeth in an angry manner. The first student who can correctly guess the right word then has a chance to have a go at doing the mime themselves. It should be feasible for all students to have a go at this activity. The focus here is clearly on recognising other people's feelings and emotions, i.e. developing empathy and particularly observing facial expression, body language and demeanour.

Daniel's Letters

The facilitator then reads the third of Daniel's Letters in which he describes his second day at the Pupil Referral Unit. Daniel describes how he had an altercation with another child in the cookery lesson because he wasn't able to wait his turn. This was extremely upsetting for all involved and results in Daniel being put on a special report card. He is asked to identify with his teacher three specific targets which include: waiting his turn, not losing his temper and going to get the teacher if he feels either of those things happening to him. Daniel is finding it an increasingly more complex place to be and is particularly concerned that because the PRU is a smaller place than his mainstream school, he can't get away with anything. He is quite honest about this in the letter and says, 'I can't pretend it was someone else because there were too many witnesses.' It seems to be that the teachers can actually monitor the behaviour more effectively because they are more on top of it and there are fewer kids to actually look after.

The facilitator reads the following letter:

Dear Friend,

Today was my second day at the Pupil Referral Unit. Miss Jones, our teacher, is really quite kind. When I got in there she made me sit and talk to her for ten minutes and she went through why everything had gone wrong the day before at playtime. She said if I was to get angry or feel that I was getting angry again, I needed to come and find her straight away. I needed to be able to walk away and hold my breath and all that sort of thing. I looked at her and I thought she's nice. I didn't want to tell her I have tried all that and it just doesn't work. At least it doesn't work for me that is. It's almost like I need something else. I need someone to be holding my hands behind my back and stopping me somehow. It's like I can't stop myself yet. I tried to say something to her but she didn't really understand. She seemed to think that if I kept going at it I would just get better. Maybe she is right. I hope she is anyway.

So today was quite good really. That's what my mum said anyway. She said you must think about all the bits that went well and that if there are more of them than the ones that didn't, then you have had a good day. So I suppose more went well than went bad. The funny thing about being at PRU is that you don't just get taught by your one teacher, other people come in and do things with you as well because they have got all the older ones. We don't really see the older children because we are in a separate block but they are all there too so they have got special teachers like the cookery one. We went to her today. She is really pretty. She has got long blonde hair and really long legs. She looks like a model or a film star and she is very kind but she is very strict. We all have to wash our hands about three times in every lesson and if she catches anyone picking their nose she goes bananas. She went mad at Ben, the little one, because he was putting his finger in his ear and then he was doing his cooking and she said, 'Do you really think that anyone would want to eat that after you have done that!' Anyway, he went off and washed his hands so he was alright after that but I did think about it – ear wax and bogies wouldn't be very nice in your shepherds pie would they?

Anyway things were going well in that cookery lesson until we had to do something which meant we had to wait our turn for the spoon. There is a special spoon, she only had one of them. When you fry the meat you put the spoon in, scoop out the meat and all the fat drains off and you need to do it because otherwise your shepherd's pie will be too fatty. Anyway, I had to wait in line and of course it's the one thing that I find really difficult because I wanted to go first to get it over with. It's boring just standing there waiting, especially when the fat boy in front of me found it so hard and he kept spilling bits. I could feel myself getting really angry at him. When he did it for the third time I'd just had enough so I snatched the spoon off him and said, 'Let me go first because I am quicker than you.' Anyway that was it, another blow.

Anyway, I got sent out and I had to sit outside the headteacher's office for five minutes. When he came out and asked me what was wrong I just told him the truth. I thought it's no good lying here. I couldn't pretend it was someone else because there were too many witnesses. It's too small a place. That's what I am finding out. You can't get away with things so much here because there are so few of you and there are so many of them, that, they see what you do all the time. Anyway I'd lost it, I knew that for sure, so I just admitted it. Now they have put me on this behaviour thing. I have got this special record sheet and I have to try and get 10 points each day.

The main target is to wait my turn; my second target is not to lose my temper; my third target is to go and get the teacher if I feel either of those things happening to me. Sounds easy. I don't think it will be. Anyway, I will have to let you know how I get on because I am running out of ink now. In fact my hand's aching so I am not writing any more today. I will write again tomorrow and let you know how my third day goes.

All the best,

Daniel

Questions for discussion

- How do you think Daniel felt about his second day at the PRU and why?

- What was different about lessons at the PRU compared to his mainstream school?

- What happened in the cookery lesson?

- What do you think about Daniel's behaviour towards the boy in the queue?

- What do you think Daniel could have done differently?

- How do you think Daniel's behaviour needs to change? Do you think anyone else needs to help him?

- What kind of a report card would you want for Daniel? Can you have a go at making one up? Make sure you consider the kinds of rewards that he might like to have.

- What rewards do you have in your classroom and how does this system work for you? Would it work for Daniel too?

Worksheet activities - 'Think Funny' and 'Anger Diary'

There are two worksheet activities for this session. The first is entitled 'Think Funny'. The students are asked to think of things that make them laugh and to record these on the sheet. The idea here is to introduce them to the concept of distraction i.e. if we start to feel angry we can very often prevent the feeling from escalating still further by distracting ourselves through humour, i.e. thinking funny.

The second worksheet takes the form of an Anger Diary. The students are asked to record the feelings they experience on a daily basis for a one week period. It is hoped that the subsequent reflection process will then help them to recognise and avoid the most common or significant triggers in the future.

Plenary

In the plenary session the facilitator can once again summarise the main concepts covered in the session and reinforce key learning points. It may also be helpful to reinforce the class reward system and to gather students' views as to how effective they think it is for each of them. This may lead to a revision of the system and the making of more appropriate rewards for individual students within the group at this time.

Think Funny

Sometimes we can help ourselves by thinking of something funny when we first get that little bit of anger. What makes you laugh? What can you think of?

Record your answers in the speech bubbles below.

Anger Diary

Record your feelings on each day of the week. Think carefully about things that made you feel angry and why this happened.

Discuss with your teacher or helper.

Monday

Tuesday

Wednesday

Thursday

Friday

Saturday

Sunday

Look out for the triggers!

Session 4

Dealing with Things People Say

Warm-up activity – 'Copycats'

In this game the facilitator can start the activity by producing some kind of action, e.g. handclapping, tapping, stamping of feet, making actions or mimes in the air. The rest of the group are required to follow these actions. When the facilitator shouts 'Pass', the movements move to the person on his or her left-hand side. That person then has to start making movements themselves and the rest of the group have to copy. The idea here is to make the movements as complicated and quick as possible so as to ensure that everyone in the group is really concentrating and listening properly.

Daniel's Letters

The facilitator then reads the fourth of Daniel's Letters which describes a special outing that the group went on in order to gain and develop cooperative skills and social skills. This involved the building of structures. Daniel works really well with his partner and produces one of the best structures and both of the boys are really pleased because they know that they are going to get a special prize. However, as they are clearing up to go to lunch, another boy is very rude to them and starts to accuse them of being gay, saying, 'You two fancy each other.' Unfortunately, this causes Daniel to lose his temper with both of the boys who seem to be bullying him and he jumps on them and starts to lash out. He has totally lost his temper. This is not a good end to the week for him. However, he is once again surprised when he goes back to the PRU and the headteacher is very, very upset at his behaviour but also makes sure that Daniel realises that next week is a fresh week and a new start. It seems unusual to Daniel that the teachers can have so much empathy for him and can understand exactly why this would cause him to lose his temper.

The facilitator reads the following letter:

Dear Friend,

So much has happened since I last wrote to you that I'm not sure where to start. On Friday, at the end of my first week at the PRU, something really good happened. Our teacher, Miss Jones, and the headteacher, Mr Morris, took us all out on a special trip. Usually you only get trips if you have done really well or you've done good work or you've not hit people – I know that from my last school – but it seems to be different here. Mr Morris said that we were going out on a special trip because we needed to learn how to work together as a team and that meant going out and doing some things together as a group. He said that learning how to cooperate was one of the most important skills people could have in life. I wasn't sure what he meant until we actually started to do it all.

We went off in the school van about 9:30am and we drove right down to where the older kids do the water skiing. I was watching some of them out on the water and I felt quite jealous. I would have liked to have gone water skiing but you can only do that when you are in Years 9 and 10. Anyway, to get back to where I was, what we were doing was called cooperative games. We had to get together in pairs first of all and work out how we were going to build a shelter. We were given some string, nails, and a hammer and told to walk into the wood where a clearing had been made for us. It looked like someone had come in and bashed down all the trees for about 30 square metres. That meant that there was loads of stuff by the side that we could go and pick up. Anyway, the winners were going to be the people or the pairs who could finish first and build the strongest structure. That's what Mr Morris said. I was told to go and work with Harry which I was quite pleased about because he seems OK – at least he hasn't said anything that could make me get angry and he doesn't give people dirty looks either.

Anyway, it was brilliant. We worked really, really, well together and Mr Morris said he was proud of us because we built the best structure. He went round testing them all and out of the four that we had, ours was the best even though two of them had had teachers working with them. We knew we were going to get a special prize. It was great. The trouble was that then the problems started.

As we were walking away from our dens to go and get our lunch, two of the other kids in the group started making funny noises like they were pigs or something. I turned around and looked at them and I said to the one boy, 'What are you doing that for?' He just grinned at me and started to make grunting pig noises again. I knew what he was trying to do – he was trying to get me angry. I could feel my triggers going but I kept thinking, 'No, I've got to keep calm, I've got to keep calm, I mustn't react to him.' The problem was they were saying things like, 'Your mum smells,' but it was when they actually said, 'You two fancy each other,' to me and

Harry that I saw red. That was it. I just lost it – I wasn't going to take that in front of other pupils.

I jumped on both of them and I started lashing out. It was like the same old me again. I was just angry, angry, angry. It was bad. Mr Morris had to come and split us up and by accident I thumped him. It really was an accident 'cause I was trying to aim for the other kid but he got in the way so I hit him in the stomach. He went red in the face. Anyway it was a bad end because we all had to go back to the PRU. We weren't allowed to stay any longer so we had to eat our sandwiches in the coach going back and then my mum got called up and it was the usual thing – like I wasn't doing well enough and I'd lost it. Mind you, I have to say they were alright about me hitting the teacher because they knew that was an accident so that made me feel a bit better. I just had to say sorry to people. It was a bad end to the week but the good thing about it was that the headteacher kept saying, 'Look, next week it's a new week, it's a new start so just go in there and be positive and try again.' At least they are willing to give me another chance. I just hope that I can hold on to it a bit more next week. I think what I've got to learn to do is just ignore nasty things people say and think of something I can do to get back at them without using my fists.

Yours,

Daniel

Questions for discussion

- Why do you think that the teachers arranged for the pupils to do cooperative tasks?

- What were Harry and Daniel building in the woods?

- Why was Mr Morris so pleased with them?

- What did the other kids start doing when they were walking over to eat lunch?

- Why did Daniel lose his temper again?

- What do you think he should have done in order to stop getting angry at them?

- What would you do if this happened to you?

- How would you respond in order to get the best possible outcome?

Worksheet activity – 'Things People Say'

The students are asked to reflect upon the things that people say to them that can make them feel angry. They are required to write down the words that make them feel most angry and to then write down what they could 'do' or 'say' in order to stop themselves getting so angry. Once again, it may be helpful to provide an opportunity for students to share their strategies.

Plenary

The facilitator can reinforce the key skills covered in the session and particularly emphasise the students' 'personal' anger management strategies. It may be useful to record these on a whiteboard and to then encourage students to try out a new strategy during the coming week.

Things People Say

Things people say can make us feel angry – especially if they cuss us or our families. Write down in the cards the words that make you feel most angry and then write down what you could do or say in order to stop yourself getting angry back.

They say

I say/do

They say

I say/do

They say

I say/do

They say

I say/do

Session 5

Learning to Relax

Warm-up activity – 'Moving places'

In this game the students are asked to change places within the circle if they are wearing, thinking or feeling certain things. For example, if the facilitator says, 'Change places if you are wearing something white', then all those who are wearing something white will have to change places. This can then be further adapted, e.g. change places if you are feeling sad today, change places if you lost your temper last week, change places if you managed to use an anger management strategy. Obviously this is not only useful for reinforcing skills and strategies that the students have developed but is also a fun game in which they can become more aware of each other's space and the need to move around carefully within the classroom context.

Daniel's Letters

The facilitator then reads the fifth of Daniel's Letters which describes his first day of the second week at the Pupil Referral Unit. Daniel seems to feel really happy now and is getting far more relaxed and able to cope with the curriculum. He also particularly enjoyed the work with the creative arts therapist which he describes in some detail. This involves making use of relaxation strategies and techniques. However, on a negative note, Daniel is starting to consider how he can manage to keep himself at the PRU as he doesn't really want to go back to a mainstream school. He thinks to himself that if he doesn't behave all the time and he is a bit bad sometimes then they might have to keep him.

The facilitator reads the following letter:

Dear Friend,

Today was my first day of the second week at the PRU and, for the first time, I think I have had a really brilliant day. It wasn't that I was dead good all the time – it was just that I managed not to lose it at all. I was able to do the walking away and the time out and the things that I have been told to a bit more. It did seem to work a bit. I was able to keep myself calm when someone gave me a dirty look and I was able not to even answer back when someone said something nasty under their breath about me.

The real reason it was such a good day though was because we had this special teacher come in. She was really brilliant. She said she was a Creative Arts Therapist (whatever that is) but what she really was, was someone who would make us think about ourselves a bit more and try and relax and not get stressed by stuff. She said that kids get just as stressed as adults. I have never heard an adult say that before. Normally they tell you just to forget about your problems but she said the worries that we have are just as big and significant as the worries that adults have. I don't know if my mum would agree with that because she is always worried about money and I don't have to be worried about money. But then I am worried about people thinking I am thick and stupid and I am worried about my school and I am worried about not being able to see my dad. This lady (her name was Alison), she said that those worries were just as significant. Anyway, we had to sit round in a circle and we all had to say what things we felt bad about, what things we felt guilty about, what things we felt happy about and stuff like that. It was quite hard because you didn't want to say much in front of the others but she said it was really important that we kept all the stuff in the room confidential and that people were not told what we were talking about. She said it was our private room and it was our private time to relax. What we had to do was be friends with each other and help each other so that we could get back to mainstream school.

I don't know if I want to go back to mainstream school now. It seems really nice here. You get tea and toast in the morning and then we have the relaxing stuff with her which is really nice and then we do art and then cookery again. 'Why do I want to go back to another school?' Maybe if I don't behave all the time and I'm a bit bad sometimes, they'll have to keep me here. Anyway, I have to tell you the bit about the relaxing – it was brilliant.

We all had to lie on the floor and pretend that we were going to sleep. We had to lie there and feel ourselves going to sleep from the bottom of our toes right to the tips of our fingers and up to our head. We had to feel every muscle relax in our bodies. It was brilliant. In the background she played music. It was calming. It wasn't the sort of music I normally like but the funniest bit of all was that our teacher, Miss Jones, went to sleep. We saw her shut her eyes as she was on her mat and she started to snore. Well, we laughed like mad. We thought it was brilliant. Alison had to wake her up but I just laughed and laughed. And you know, the nice thing was that when she woke up, she just laughed as well. She said, 'I've had a big weekend, that's why. Sorry guys.' Anyway, at the end of this day I really think that the PRU is a good place to be. I didn't lose it and I enjoyed it – it was great. I like all the stuff we do. I like the fact the teachers listen and they don't blame you all the time. I like the fact that they don't think I'm so bad which makes me think I'd better start being a bit bad because otherwise they won't let me stay here, they'll make me go back to a mainstream school and I don't want that. I don't think I could manage. I don't think I could be good again with loads of other kids in the room and it's nice here. I feel safe.

Yours,

Daniel

Questions for discussion

- How do you think Daniel was feeling when he went back into the PRU for the start of the second week?

- What were the main reasons that hc had such a good day?

- How did Alison teach the pupils how to relax?

- Why do you think Daniel is more able to control his behaviour and not react badly when people make him feel angry?

- Why does he think he might have to start being badly behaved again?

- What is he frightened of?

- Do you think things will be difficult for him if he goes back to a mainstream school – if so, why?

- What kinds of things do you think would help him get back to a mainstream school?

- How do you feel about going back to a new mainstream school?

- What do you think would help you?

Worksheet activity – 'Relax, Don't Do It'

Students are asked to consider how they relax and how their friends and family relax. They are also asked to identify what healthy things they can do in order to relax effectively. They are asked to discuss their ideas with a friend and to record their ideas in the thought bubbles on the worksheet. It may be helpful to share ideas during the plenary session or to allocate some further time to this in order to reinforce the most healthy and positive ways in which students can relax and de-stress throughout different times of the week.

Optional exercise – 'Relax - Try It'

The facilitator may wish to introduce and try out a relaxations script with the group. This script is taken from *Escape from Exclusion*.

Plenary

The facilitator can once again reinforce the key skills covered in this particular session. It will also be an opportunity for students to voice any of their concerns or fears about going back to a mainstream school. These can be brainstormed, perhaps in a series of myths and realities, e.g. what is the myth? If you go back to a mainstream school it may be that nobody will like you there because they know you were excluded before. What is the reality? The reality is that everyone will be making an effort to try and keep you in the school because the teachers would not have given you the place unless they thought that you could manage.

Relax, Don't Do It

We can help ourselves by learning how to relax. How do we relax?
How do your friends and family relax? What are healthy things to do?
Discuss with a friend and record your ideas in the thought bubbles.

Relax – Try It

Choose a quiet room and a time when you're unlikely to be disturbed.

Wear very light clothing.

Lie on your back on the floor or a firm surface.

Tense the muscles in your right foot and ankle. Wriggle your toes. How does it feel? Clench the muscles and release them several times. Notice the difference in sensation between the clenched and unclenched muscles. Commit it to memory.

Repeat the exercises with your left foot and ankle.

Tense the calf muscles, first one then the other. Repeat several times, alternately clenching and unclenching. Once again notice the differences in sensation between the tense and the relaxed state. Remember it.

Move next to the thigh muscles, and carry out the same exercise. Notice how tension in the thighs affects the kneecaps and the knees.

Work upwards, taking in the muscles of the abdomen, of the chest, and of the back and shoulders, working upon each group in turn.

Now work on the biceps, the forearms and the hands.

Lastly, move to the neck, the jaw and the forehead, and the scalp.

Session 6

Coping with Loss and Taking Time Out

Warm-up activity – 'I went shopping'

The facilitator starts by saying, 'I went shopping and I bought…' This sentence then gets passed around the whole of the circle so that each student can add an item of shopping to the list. By the time it gets to the last student in the circle there will be quite a long sentence to remember. This is quite a fun game, however, and the students generally enjoy it. They can be encouraged to make use of visual cues and to try and visualise the item with the person as they go round the circle. This strategy does seem to help some individuals to retain the information. Once they become more skilled at the game, it can be possible to go round the circle two or three times depending upon the size of the group.

Daniel's Letters

The facilitator can read Daniel's Letter for Session 6. In this letter, Daniel describes how one member of his class has experienced a bereavement. He went home to find that his mum had died of an overdose. This obviously causes Daniel and the rest of the group some level of distress and they are supported through this process by the school psychologist. Daniel decides that he will write a letter to Harry in order to say how sorry he feels for him and also decides to keep his temper when Harry returns to the class because he feels that he has already been through enough without having to cope with other people's bad behaviour being directed at him.

The facilitator reads the following letter:

Dear Friend,

I didn't write to you yesterday because I was too sad. Something really horrible happened at the PRU. We all went into the classroom as normal in the morning and Miss Jones set out our tea and toast while we were doing quiet reading. It started like a normal day. It was quiet and everyone seemed OK. No one was really coming in angry or anything. Then I realised that Harry hadn't come in. He was late. His taxi had gone to pick him up and Miss said he wasn't ready so he would be in a bit later. I felt a bit angry at the time because we were supposed to both be working on our write up of the Activity Day together. We were making a joint book and if he wasn't there, I would have to do all the writing which really I wasn't that happy about because it isn't that easy for me. Not that I'm saying I'm not good at writing but I'm not the best so I was a bit fed up with it. Anyway, we had just started doing our literacy lesson when the headteacher came over. He whispered something to the teacher and took her outside. They seemed to be out there for ages. When they came back in he told all of us to put down our pencils and to come into the other room where we could sit like we do for Circle Time in the big soft chairs. We all went through. We were like wondering what was going on. Harry still wasn't there.

Anyway, the headteacher had spoken to Harry and Harry had given him permission to tell us what had happened. He had gone home the night before and when he walked in there was a big problem. He had found his mum lying on the floor and they had to rush her to hospital because it looked as though she wasn't breathing. The guy that takes Harry in the taxi was really upset. He took Harry in then went to phone the ambulance and the police and everything. Harry had to go in the ambulance with them to hospital and then what they found was that his mum had taken a drugs overdose. She had got really upset and had just taken loads and loads of pills. She had the ones that you take to go to sleep and she had taken too many. Then the headteacher said that we all had to hope that Harry was OK because what had happened in the end was that his mum had died. She seemed to go to sleep and then didn't wake up again. He said that the main thing was that she wasn't in pain and she didn't suffer because she had been unconscious.

Harry has been sent away. He's been sent to stay with his gran and there is a Social Worker, the one that two of the other kids have got. She has gone to the house as well. We were all shocked – none of us knew what to say. I felt like crying and I couldn't think of him not having his mum because it made me think of not having my mum and how I would just crack up without her even though she gets angry at me. I know she loves me and I know I love her. It was like thinking of someone not having someone to love them like that. It must be bad.

Anyway, this psychologist person came in. We had not seen him before but he sat down with us and we all had to sit and say how we felt about things which I thought was a bit stupid because we didn't know him so I'd rather have talked to my teacher really. But anyway, then he did this thing where we all had to draw pictures of how we felt and think about things we could do to help Harry so I thought I would write him a letter. It was short because I didn't know what to say but I put my picture in with it and my picture was of me and him. I also put in a photo of us that Mr Morris had taken when we were making our camp. I thought that would help him because I said, 'You know you have still got me as your friend and I'll be there for you.' I didn't know what else to say really. I didn't want to sound soft or wet. Everyone was sad though – the whole school. It felt funny, like the whole building was sad. The teachers all looked upset too. I've never had anyone die apart from my pet rat. That was bad enough but I think that if it's your mum I don't know what you would do, I don't know what I would do. It must be really bad.

I don't want to write any more because I don't know what to say. I wonder what it will be like tomorrow. What will everyone be saying and when will Harry get back? I hope he comes back to school soon but Miss Jones seems to think that he's going to need some time at home. She said some people take a long time to get over it, some people don't, but she said he would need our help when he gets back. It made me think about how angry I'd got with him when I first got to the PRU. I felt guilty. I must try to keep my temper now because I couldn't hurt him, not when he has been through this bad time.

Yours,

Daniel

Questions for discussion

- Why was Daniel a little bit upset at the start of the day?

- What do you think the pupils felt like when they saw the headteacher come into the room?

- How do you think the headteacher felt when he had to tell the pupils about Harry?

- How did Daniel feel when he found out about Harry's mum?

- Why did the psychologist come in to see the pupils?

- What did Daniel do for Harry at this point?

- Why do you think Harry will need to take some time out of school?

- How do you think the other pupils can help him when he gets back to the PRU?

- Sometimes we take time out if we're feeling angry but sometimes we might need to take time out for other things. What other things would you need to take time out for?

Worksheet activity – 'Taking Time Out'

The students are asked to identify times when they might need to make use of this strategy and to consider what they could do at these times, i.e. what would be the best thing for them to do and why.

Plenary

In the plenary session the facilitator can once again reinforce the concepts and issues covered in this session. It may be helpful to ask students for personal feedback in terms of their use of time out facilities. It may also be useful to consider ways of supporting people who have been bereaved or lost someone or something significant. This may well be an experience common to many of the students in the group and will need to be addressed with some sensitivity. It may be useful for the facilitator to record students' views and ideas as to how they can support one another should such events occur in their lives.

Taking Time Out

When do you need to take time out?

List the times:

What can you do in these times? List your ideas.

What would be the best thing for you to do and why?

Time Out

Session 7
Talking Through Problems

Warm-up activity – 'Vikings'

This game involves the students sitting in a circle as for Circle Time. The facilitator nominates a Viking Chief. He or she must row a longship whilst making 'heave ho' noises (miming). The player on either side of the Viking Chief should then row with the arm nearest to the Chief, making the same noise. When the Chiefton wishes to pass on her duties, she should stand up and, making a blowing noise, shoot an imaginary arrow at her choice of the new Chiefton. The new Chiefton then takes up rowing duties and the player to his immediate left begins with single-handed strokes. Anyone within the group who doesn't take up the challenge is out, along with those using the wrong arm. The game continues until there are three players left and then these are identified as the winners.

Daniel's Letters

In this letter Daniel describes how he is experiencing some bullying. Instead of reacting in a violent or aggressive way, he has actually become rather withdrawn. He has resisted the temptation to hit out or fight the boy concerned but is becoming increasingly intimidated to the extent where he feels like not going into school the next day. He describes how he hasn't told anyone and simply doesn't know what to do.

The facilitator reads the letter entry as follows:

Dear Friend

Well, I've now been at the PRU for three weeks. I haven't written for a few days because I've been feeling quite fed up. It's not all bad but there's enough bad to make me feel fed up. It all started last Friday as we were finishing off for the day and packing up our things ready to take home. I went to get my reading book and my weekly record to give to my mum. As I was walking over to my tray, Basil, who only came to the PRU two days earlier, decided that he'd try and trip me up. I saw him stick out his foot and I managed to get round it. He just looked at me and started to laugh and said, 'Just wait 'til later – I'll get you.' I thought I'd just ignore him. We'd been practising ignoring all week so I thought I'd better have a go and it's one of my targets on my target sheet. But it wasn't easy – I felt really angry. I could feel myself getting hot and I knew I wanted to say something back to him. I didn't though – I just looked at him and walked back to my desk. Miss Jones didn't see it. I don't think anyone else did.

Anyway, over the weekend I thought about it a bit. I didn't say anything to my mum because I though she'd get upset if she thought there was anything going on. When I was at my last school I was always accused of bullying other kids and picking on them. Every time that something went wrong, it was like it was my fault and that's what the teacher said – it was me that was doing it or starting on others. I knew that wasn't always true. The problem was that if someone did say something to me, I always reacted back and punched them before they punched me because I thought if I didn't, they'd just bully me. The problem was that even then, I did actually get bullied by two different people – one of them was a Year 6 boy and the other one was his brother outside of school. They decided to pick on me because I thumped his brother once and hurt him really badly. That went on for a bit but no one believed me so I just gave up saying anything.

I thought about it over the weekend and decided that I'd just ignore it and forget about it. I thought the best thing to do would be to come back on the Monday and not tell anyone anything. He probably would have forgotten about it as well. I didn't know why he was starting because I hadn't done anything to him. In fact, I'd been quite nice to him when he arrived on the Wednesday because I knew what it felt like so I'd made friends with him and taken him round and showed him where the toilets were and the PE stuff – everything.

So, I went back into school and thought no more about it. That was until he came into the classroom late on the Monday. He gave me one of those looks – you know, the ones that kids do when they have trodden in something and they're saying that's what you are, some dirt under their foot – then he made a signal with his hand as if he was strangling himself and pointed at me laughing. Before he did it he made sure no one was looking so it was only me that saw. I looked down at my work and thought for a bit. I could either thump him at break time or I could just carry on ignoring it. The problem was that by ignoring it I was feeling more and more scared.

When it got to break time, Miss Jones came out to supervise us and I decided I'd stay pretty near to her when we were playing, just in case. But nothing happened. Basil just kept on looking at me giving me sly glances. Then it happened. He decided to cuss my mum. He started saying really, really nasty things about her under his breath every time be walked past me. This went on for the whole of the rest of the day. When it got to the end of the day I'd had enough and I said to him, 'If you say one more thing, I'm going to punch you.' He looked at me and started to laugh and said, 'You're just a wimp – you wouldn't punch me – you're a sissy – you can't fight.' And you know, for once I thought I couldn't. I really felt like crying. I didn't want to admit it but I just thought there was something so nasty about the way he was looking at me. He was making me feel really, really small.

Anyway, it's got to the stage now where I don't want to go in tomorrow. I haven't told anybody. I don't know what to do. I just feel like I can't go in and face it anymore.

Yours,

Daniel

Questions for discussion

- Why had Daniel not written to his letters for so long?

- When did he first notice that he was being bullied?

- What was happening?

- How do you think he felt after the first bullying incident?

- Do you think that Daniel was right to ignore Basil's behaviour?

- What was the worst bit of bullying that Daniel had to cope with?

- Why do you think he didn't fight back?

- What do you think Daniel should have done to help himself?

- What would you do if you were being bullied?

- What happens in the PRU if someone is bullying someone else?

- Where do you go to for help?

Worksheet activity – 'Talk Time'

Students are introduced to the notion of 'talking through' problems with a friend. The questions on the worksheet provide them with a problem-solving format which will hopefully enable them to formulate an appropriate solution.

Plenary

The facilitator can summarise the main points covered in this session and particularly focus upon the kinds of things that students can do to help and support each other when they have experienced a loss. It will be important to emphasise how different people react in very different ways and that the most important thing is to listen and to understand what each individual needs, i.e. not forcing attention on someone who simply wants to be quiet and take time out for themselves. It will also be important to reinforce the usefulness of the problem-solving format to encourage students to make use of this in the future.

Talk Time

When you feel angry or have a problem, it's a good idea to talk it through with a friend. Use the following list of questions in order to interview each other and try to help each other find a solution.

What is the problem?

How do you feel?

How do you think the other person(s) feels?

What would make you feel better?

What would make the other person(s) feel better?

What are your options?

Which is the best and why?

Go on! Try it out!

Session 8

Using 'I' Messages

Warm-up activity – 'The Whispering Game'

One person begins by whispering a sentence to the person directly to their left. The sentence is then repeated around the circle until the last person, who has to say the sentence out loud.

Daniel's Letters

In this letter Daniel describes how the situation with the boy who is bullying him is sorted out.

The teacher describes how people who bully are generally scared themselves and both Basil and Daniel are asked to consider each other's feelings and to learn how to empathise more with each other.

The facilitator reads the following letter:

Dear Friend,

Well, you will be glad to know that all the stuff with Basil has been sorted out now and it was me being stupid – that's why it didn't get sorted out. I know what I should have done. I should have gone and told the teacher straight away. Anyway, the reason she found out wasn't because of me. I didn't really do the right thing and go and tell her. It was because two of the other kids (the older ones) saw something in the playground and they reported it. Once that had happened I had to confess to how long it had been going on.

Miss Jones got us to sit down separately with her and got both sides of the story. It was quite funny really because Basil said that he didn't really mean to bully me – he said he'd just got so used to having to be nasty to people because if he wasn't nasty to them they tended to bully him. At least that's what he said had happened to him in his old school. I think I understood that. It's like you get in first before someone hurts you. He said he was sorry for bullying me and he would never do it again. I said it was alright – I did understand it but he had hurt my feelings and I really didn't like the stuff he'd said about my mum. Miss Jones says people only bully other people because they're scared themselves. She said did I understand about how he felt coming into the PRU being new and the newest one to the whole group. I said that I did understand that because it's how I felt. You are scared at first and I suppose that makes you feel jumpy so you are more likely to pounce on other people. It is hard. Anyway, things are much better now. We decided that we would just forget about it. Miss Jones said '…put a veil over it' whatever that means.

Miss Jones also gave us a special lesson. She said that what we needed to do was learn about using 'I' messages. It was about saying how we felt and how we wanted people to stop doing things if we got upset instead of walking up to them and punching them because they had said something nasty to you. She wanted us to practise saying things like, 'I don't like you saying that. I think it's horrible and I'm going to go for help now.' It felt a bit like doing a play in one of our drama lessons but we all had to practise it in turns – one person being the bully and one person being the bullied person – and practise being what she called assertive, not in an aggressive way so no shouting or thumping or anything like that and definitely no swearing. So Basil and I paired up together. We had quite a laugh – it was good. I think at the end of it I have learnt how to use 'I' messages. I think it might help me in the future, especially when I go back to mainstream school because the more I can do it, the better I'll get at it and then the less likely I am to lose my temper again – at least I hope that's true!

Because we did so well, Miss Jones gave us extra playtime. She is good like that. That's why it's nice here – it's not the same as a mainstream school where you just have to stick to the rules all the time. Here, if you've been really, really good, she can just give you an extra ten minutes play. You couldn't do that in my old school because the other kids would get jealous and the teachers would get angry with each other for showing favouritism. Here it's great because no one says anything. We are the only class of juniors here anyway – the other kids are all older and they're in the bigger building.

When I went home and told my mum about the 'I' messages she was really interested. She said it's funny because she thinks she could use some of that in her work. 'It would help me,' she said, 'if I felt people were trying to give me too much to do and I couldn't do it. I think I need to be more assertive like that as well. They teach you good stuff in that PRU, don't they?' 'I think they do,' I said. Anyway, I'll write again soon.

Yours,

Daniel

Questions for discussion

- Why did Daniel feel better when he wrote to his friend this time?

- How had he and Basil sorted out the situation?

- Why was Basil so defensive to start with?

- How do you think he felt when he first came to the Pupil Referral Unit?

- Did Daniel understand what was happening to Basil?

- Why would cussing your mum be more hurtful than anything else?

- Do you agree that it is, if so why?

- Can you use 'I' statements?

- Have you ever been taught how to?

- Do you think that Daniel really likes the PRU now and, if so, why?

- What is so different about it or special?

- Why was Daniel's mum so pleased?

- How do you think Daniel feels now and why?

Worksheet activity – 'Using 'I' Messages'

We are asked to consider the ways in which using 'I' messages help us to respond positively to a difficult situation. The facilitator may need to clarify this concept at the outset and to focus upon the ways in which being assertive can help us in very tricky complex situations. Saying how you feel works better than showing your anger by hitting out. Students are asked to think of five situations that make them feel angry and to then make up an 'I' message for each one. It may be helpful to get students to practice using these 'I' messages in pairs by a role-playing activity subsequent to completion of the worksheet.

Plenary

The facilitator can describe the main points covered in the session and also highlight the importance of being assertive and coping with the bullying behaviour of others. It will be important to reinforce this concept of using 'I' messages and to encourage students to make use of this technique in the coming weeks.

Using 'I' Messages

Using 'I' messages helps us to respond positively to difficult situations. Remember – saying how you feel works better than showing your anger by hitting out. Think of five situations that make you feel angry. Then make up an 'I' message for each one.

Situation 1
'I' message:

Situation 2
'I' message:

Situation 3
'I' message:

Situation 4
'I' message:

Situation 5
'I' message:

Session 9

Problem-solving using Traffic Lights

Warm-up activity – 'Sharks'

In this game the facilitator can lay out a few hoops or draw chalk circles – whatever is appropriate within the classroom context. The hoops are described as islands within a shark infested area. The students are asked to walk around the hoops, not standing still or hanging around. The facilitator then shouts out 'sharks' and all the students have to take refuge in a hoop. Any children who are caught by the shark (one child nominated by the facilitator to travel around and tap children on the side) are then out of the game. The facilitator gradually pulls out hoops throughout the activity so that the students have to manage to manoeuvre themselves into one hoop by the end of the session. The idea of this game is that they are encouraged to help each other and cooperate with each other in order to stay in the hoop.

Daniel's Letters

In this letter Daniel talks about how his time at the PRU is coming to an end and how he is feeling sad and scared about leaving. He has an interview with the headteacher and his mum tells how she has found some of the advice that has been given to Daniel helpful too.

Even though Daniel is worried about going back to mainstream school, he decides that he is willing to 'go for it'.

The facilitator reads the following letter:

Dear Friend,

This is probably going to be my last letter to you for a bit because things are changing quite a lot now. I am coming towards the end of my time at the PRU. I've only got, like, two weeks to go before they send me back to school. It doesn't seem that long to me. It seems such a short time. Maybe it's because I've liked it here. I didn't like it so much at first but now I feel like I'm not sure if I want to go back to school or not.

Yesterday I had a special interview with the headteacher. I had to go through all the different things that I had learnt while I had been here and I had to say how I felt about everything. My mum came in as well. It was like a special review meeting. They filled in this big long chart – it said 'Reintegration Readiness Scale.' Apparently I scored over 70 points on it so it looks as though I've got to go back to mainstream school. My mum was really pleased. She sat there and smiled quite a lot, especially when the headteacher said all the different things I had learnt. He said I was much better at controlling my temper; that I could show that I cared for other people, and I had also learnt how to control my behaviour better. I could stop and think before acting and I could control my feelings if I got angry in particular. That's been the hardest bit. There were some blips. There were about three incident reports on me for losing my temper but he said it was a big improvement and much better than when I came in originally. The bit my mum liked best was when they said about learning assertiveness skills and using 'I' messages. She laughed. She said to the headteacher, 'Well, I looked at all his worksheets and things that he brought home and I learnt how to do that as well and it has helped me too.' I felt proud of my mum. Normally she wouldn't look so pleased. I think I've made her feel miserable for a long time now but she looked happy today in that meeting. It made me feel good too.

Anyway, the headteacher asked me how I felt about going back. I looked at him and I tried to smile but actually I felt quite sad. I also felt a bit sick inside. I'm scared that I won't be able to cope and that I'll let everyone down again and I'm also scared that the teachers will just get at me again and won't give me a second chance. I think that he knew that. He turned to me and he smiled and said, 'Well, it's a new school – it's a fresh start and everybody deserves another chance.' I'm just worried because it's alright here where there are just six of us in the class but I'm scared that I won't be able to cope when I go back in. I did tell him the truth a bit and then I said, 'What would happen if I was bad again? Say I started to be bad here, then you'd have to keep me here, wouldn't you?' He said no he wouldn't. He said that's not allowed. He said you are supposed to go back after fifteen weeks and that your time is up now. So I think I'm going to have to go for it now.

I'm going to see my new school next week. Elsie, the LSA, is taking me in. She said it will be OK because she is going to come in with me for the first four weeks. She starts off coming in for the whole week then she comes in mornings only for two weeks and then she comes in just for three afternoons the next week. 'By then', she said, 'you should be fine'. They are also going to give me a circle of friends and they are going to give me a special mentor to myself. She said I'm going to be spoilt. I hope it will be alright. Anyway, wish me good luck!

Yours

Daniel

Questions for discussion

- How long had Daniel been at the Pupil Referral Unit?

- How was he feeling now?

- What happened at the interview between him, his mum and the headteacher?

- Why was Daniel's mum so pleased? How do you think she felt?

- What was Daniel worried about?

- Who was going to help him go back to mainstream school?

- What were they going to do?

- How do you think the new teachers and his new classmates would feel about him coming?

- What advice would you give to Daniel in order to help him cope in the new situation?

- If you were in Daniel's shoes, what help would you like and how could you help yourself?

Worksheet activity – 'Traffic Lights'

The facilitator can introduce this stepped approach to problem-solving prior to asking the students to make use of it themselves. The idea here is to encourage them to adopt a stop, think and go approach to problems which uses thoughts and feelings to inform behaviour.

Plenary

The facilitator can summarise the main points covered in this session and particularly emphasise the importance of talking through difficult problems in order to find solutions and the notion of peer support and empathy being vital and crucial to such a process. It will also be helpful to emphasise the usefulness of the traffic light framework presented in the worksheet.

Traffic Lights

Use the traffic light problem-solving format to sort it out.

Stop!

What is the problem?

How do you feel?

Wait!

What can you do?

List your options

1

2

3

4

Go!

Pick your best option!

I chose option............ because ....

....

NB If it doesn't work – stop, wait and go for it again!

Session 10

Focusing on the Future and Target Setting

Warm-up activity – 'The Pea Game'

The aim of this game is for the students to collect as many peas as possible. The facilitator will need a length of rope approximately 2-3 metres long and knotted at one end to provide a framework, some dried peas and something for the students to collect the peas in, e.g. small bowls or tins. The facilitator will also need a whistle to indicate the start and end to this task. The facilitator will stand in the centre of the room with the rope. The dried peas are then spread around the facilitator in a circular area about 60cm in radius. The students are divided into pairs. Each pair is given a bowl to collect the peas in and these are arranged in four areas away from the rope which surrounds the facilitator. The facilitator then starts swinging the rope around it shin height. On the first whistle the students have to collect the peas without being hit by the rope. If they are hit they have to go out and sit away from the playing area while their team carries on. On the second whistle the players stop and count their peas. The winners are the pair of students who have the most peas.

Daniel's Letters

In this last letter, Daniel describes how he has met his targets in order to reintegrate back into a mainstream school. He is quite clear about how nervous he is feeling and is able to articulate this to his headteacher.

The facilitator reads the following letter:

Dear Friend,

This is my last letter to you. I feel quite sad about writing it in one way because it's helped me a lot to put my thoughts and feelings down on paper. At first I didn't like writing it that much but as I've gone on I've become more used to it. It's like talking to a friend. Still, I suppose I may write again at some point, you never know.

Anyway, yesterday was a very special day for me at the PRU. It was my last full day here but also I got a surprise visitor. We were doing our usual Circle Time thing that we do every Wednesday morning when two visitors were introduced to us. Our teacher just told us their names but she didn't tell us which school they came from or anything. So we all thought they were just coming to see how we do Circle Time, as other people had done that before. Anyway, afterwards, one of them called me aside and said she'd like to talk to me. She said she'd been really impressed at the way I'd contributed in the session and that I'd seemed to have had lots of sensible ideas about helping myself and other people, particularly in managing angry feelings. That's what the topic was for today. It then turned out that she is actually going to be my new teacher and her name is Miss Turner. It was really good because I hadn't noticed her watching me so I hadn't got all nervous, I was just able to be myself. She gave me a very special pack. It's called 'A Welcome Pack'. It had my name on the front of it, the name of my new school, my year group and the starting date which was properly full time from next Monday. Inside the pack there was a picture of my teacher, a picture of my class and a photo of my classroom with all the kids in it. There was also a timetable for me and every single kid in the class had written me a special letter. They had their photos included and they told me so many facts about themselves. It was really interesting and it looked like they were going to welcome me into the school.

All my worries just seemed to disappear at that moment. I couldn't quite believe that they'd gone to all that trouble. It really made me feel that they must want to have me in this new school. So all that stuff about them labelling me and making me out to be bad, like they did in my last school, is probably not true. The teacher told me all the rules and stuff but I seem to think that they're the same as the ones we've got here at the PRU. Anyway, as I've got much better at keeping them, I reckon I should be OK in my new school. When I was looking through the welcome pack at the letters from the kids I saw that at least two of them like the same things as me, exactly the same things in fact. Also, there seems to be a special teacher for Drama and Music and she does what they call relaxation sessions at lunch time. It's a bit like what we do here. I think I might be able to join in with that as well.

Anyway, hopefully, I should be OK in my new school. I still feel nervous. I still feel a bit scared but now I've seen that welcome pack and I've met my new teacher, I think I should be OK. They are not expecting me to be the most brilliant person in the world all the time. Miss Turner made that quite clear. She said we're all human beings, we all make mistakes but we all deserve to have more than one chance in the world, that's what she said. I just hope this is another good chance for me. I've got this good feeling about it though. I think it will be OK now.

Anyway, this is me signing off. I hope that you're OK. I hope that you get your wishes and that you are lucky in life as well. I'm really going to try my hardest now. I'm going to try and meet my targets and be a real success in this new school. I also think that people want me to be a success and that's half the battle isn't it, according to my mum. Anyway, see you soon. All the best.

Yours,

Daniel

Questions for discussion

- What was Daniel doing when his new teacher came to observe him in class?

- How did she feel about his contribution to the Circle Time?

- Do you think that Daniel still felt nervous about going to his new school?

- What made a difference to Daniel during this conversation?

- What kind of welcome pack would you like when you go to your new school?

- What would you include in a welcome pack and why?

- How do you think Daniel is going to do in his new school?

- Why do you think this?

- If you were in Daniel's shoes what would you think, say and do on your first day in your new school?

- What do you think would help you in your new school?

Worksheet activities -
'Strategies That Work For Me' and Going For Gold'

It may be helpful, at this point, for the facilitator to remind the students of the strategies and techniques they have learnt to date, alongside prompting individual students to share their personal strategies. The students are asked to record their self-help strategies prior to them completing the target sheet 'Going For Gold'. This final activity requires students to set themselves realistic and achievable goals for the future and to identify the strategies and resources they will need in order to meet their targets.

Plenary

The facilitator can finally support the students in revising and outlining the main topics and ideas covered within this session and particularly encourage students to focus on identifying self-help strategies and ways of coping that they may utilise once they move back into a mainstream context.

The facilitator may also wish to record the students' views as to the usefulness of the course, e.g. what has helped us? What has been less helpful? What skills have we learnt? How will we transfer our skills to a new setting? What would we change about this course in order to make it better?

Finally students can be awarded Certificates of Completion in order to celebrate their successes and involvement in the course. Alternatively, the facilitator may wish these to be presented within the context of a special assembly or award ceremony so as to publicly acknowledge and mark the students' achievements.

Strategies That Work For Me

When a strategy has worked for you, record it on a Post-it note below. Can you use it again? Go for it!

Going For Gold

Record your targets:

1.

2.

3.

What do you need to help you achieve them?

What can you do to help yourself?

What can others do to help you?

How will you know when you have reached your targets?

What will be different?

When will you review your targets?

Go for it!

Appendices

Target Card

Formats for The Welcome Pack

Course Completion Certificate

Target Card

Target Card for Daniel						
Target	Mon	Tues	Weds	Thurs	Fri	Code
1. Ignore people who make me angry						0 = need to try again.
2. Complete the task my teacher sets in the lesson						1 = tried. 2 = OK. achieved targets
3. Take time-out for 5 minutes if I feel stressed.						3 = better than expected.

Target Card						
Target	Mon	Tues	Weds	Thurs	Fri	Code
1.						0 = need to try again.
2.						1 = tried. 2 = OK achieved targets.
3.						3 = better than expected.

A Welcome Pack

For...

Name of new school: ....

Year group/class:..

Start date: ....

Hello ....

and welcome to.............................. school.

Your teacher will be: ....

Your class is called: ....

This is a photo of your classroom:

Photo

This is your new school:

Photo

This is your timetable:

Monday					
Tuesday					
Wednesday					
Thursday					
Friday					

These are the teachers in your new school:

Name ....

Class ....

A message to you:

Photo

Name ....

Class ....

A message to you:

Photo

Name ....

Class ....

A message to you:

Photo

Name ....

Class ....

A message to you:

Photo

Hello ....

My name is ....

and I am member of your new class. I have given you a list of personal points about me so that you can get to know me a bit before you come to your new school.

Facts about me:

1..................................

2..................................

3..................................

4..................................

5..................................

Photo

My special message to you is:

From ....Age...................

Hello ....

My name is ....
and I'm going to be your new teacher. I just
thought I'd tell you a bit about myself.

Facts about me:

1...................................

2...................................

3...................................

4...................................

5...................................

Photo

My special message to you is

From ....Age.................

Congratulations!

....

has completed the lessons in
Daniel's Letters

Well done! You are a star!

Signed ....

Dated...

More Books from Tina Rae

Supporting Young People Coping with Grief, Loss and Death

Tina Rae

This book has been derived from the authors research and practical work with teenagers. It focuses on the development of an emotional vocabulary, empathy, tolerance and resilience.

2006 • 128 pages
Hardback (1-4129-1311-X)
Paperback (1-4129-1312-8)

Teaching Anger Management and Problem-solving Skills for 9-12 Year Olds

Tina Rae and Brian Marris

Includes sessions built around letters from a fictional character, Daniel, allowing the participants to address typical difficulties safely.

2006 • 80 pages
Paperback (1-4129-1935-5)

Good Choices

Teaching Young People Aged 8-11 to Make Positive Decisions about Their Own Lives

Tina Rae

Provides materials to teach a course on decision making for young people aged 8-11.

2006 • 128 pages
Hardback (1-4129-1818-9)
Paperback (1-4129-1819-7)

Developing Emotional Literacy with Teenage Girls

Developing Confidence, Self-Esteem and Self-Respect

Tina Rae, Lorna Nelson and Lisa Pedersen

This 10-session programme creates an opportunity for teenage girls to be clearer and more positive about their developing identities as young women.

2005 • 96 pages
Hardback (1-4129-2049-3)
Paperback (1-4129-1905-3)

Problem Postcards

Social, Emotional and Behavioural Skills Training for Disaffected and Difficult Children aged 7-11

Janine Koeries, Brian Marris and Tina Rae

This 14-session programme is to assist young people who are disaffected and difficult, and could be at risk of exclusion.

2005 • 132 pages
Paperback (1-4129-1074-9)

Mighty Motivators

Resource Bank for Setting Targets and Rewarding Pupil Progress at Key Stage 1 & 2

Claire Moore and Tina Rae

Contains 296 printable worksheets on a CD-ROM which encourage teachers, parents or carers, and children to work together to promote positive attitudes to learning and behaviour.

2004 • 76 pages
Paperback (1-4129-1075-7)

Remembering

Providing Support for Children Aged 7 to 13 Who Have Experienced Loss and Bereavement

Lorna Nelson and Tina Rae

This resource provides a range of sensitive, positive and emotionally literate activities.

2004 • 92 pages
Paperback (1-904315-42-9)

Escape from Exclusion

An Emotionally Literate Approach to Supporting Excluded and Disaffected Students at Key Stage 2, 3 and 4

Brian Marris and Tina Rae

This 15 session emotional literacy programme assists students who are disaffected and at risk of exclusion in mainstream schools.

2004 • 156 pages
Paperback (1-904315-34-8)

Emotional Survival

An Emotional Literacy Course for High School Students

Tina Rae

The 20 lessons explore a range of feelings and provide facilitator notes and activities to help young people develop emotional literacy.

2004 • 164 pages
Paperback (1-904315-29-1)

The Anger Alphabet

Understanding Anger - An Emotional Development Programme for Young Children aged 6 to 11

Tina Rae and Karen Simmons

The 26 elements of this programme help children understand anger and to see that it is linked with other feelings such as fear, loss and jealousy.

2003 • 174 pages
Paperback (1-87394-269-9)

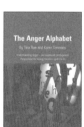

www.luckyduck.co.uk

More Books from Tina Rae

Dealing with Feeling
An Emotional Literacy Curriculum

Tina Rae

This pack of materials encouraging pupils to conduct an inner dialogue, make use of a stepped approach to solving problems, and attempt to control certain impulses.

1998 • 186 pages
Paperback (1-87394-232-X)

Dealing With Some More Feelings
An Emotional Literacy Curriculum for Children Aged 7 to 12
Book and CD

Tina Rae

Introduces 20 emotions ranging from possessive, sorry, guilty to helpful, brave and loyal in 20 whole class sessions.

2003 • 188 pages
Paperback (1-904315-03-8)

Keep Your Coooooool!
Stress Reducing Strategies for Key Stage 2 and 3
Book and CD

Tina Rae and George Robinson

'Would be a useful resource to encourage the inclusion of emotional literacy to a wider audience without "giving away" the psychology' - *Educational Psychology in Practice*

2002 • 64 pages
Paperback (1-87394-293-1)

Peter Punk
Developing Self-Esteem, Citizenship, PSHE and Literacy Skills in the Literacy Hour for Key Stages 1 and 2

Sian Deane and Tina Rae

This programme includes lesson learning intentions, stories, questions, comprehensive teacher notes, differentiated activity sheets, follow-up suggestions, cross-curricular links and plenary questions.

2002 • 276 pages
Paperback (1-87394-279-6)

School Survival
Helping Students Survive and Succeed in Secondary School

Chris Wardle and Tina Rae

Suggests practical ways to approach difficult students that may help ensure their inclusion in the mainstream context.

2002 • 140 pages
Paperback (1-87394-229-X)

Strictly Stress
Effective Stress Management: A Series of 12 Sessions for High School Students

Tina Rae

An ideal 12 session resource for helping students understand, acknowledge and cope with specific stressors.

2001 • 134 pages
Paperback (1-87394-214-1)

Confidence, Assertiveness, Self-Esteem
A Series of 12 Sessions for Secondary School Students

Tina Rae

This 12-session course teaches skills and strategies for more effective relationships and interactions at home and in school.

2000 • 182 pages
Paperback (1-87394-297-4)

Positive People
A Self-Esteem Building Course for Young Children (Key Stages 1 & 2)

Claire Moore and Tina Rae

'This handbook is likely to be a very excellent addition to resource materials available for primary phase teachers to build on their knowledge of circle time and self-esteem activities' - *Educational Psychology in Practice*

2000 • 164 pages
Paperback (1-87394-292-3)

Purr-fect Skills
A Social Skills Programme for Key Stage 1

Tina Rae

'Anyone who is committed to the development of the whole child will welcome this resource' - *SNIP*

2000 • 200 pages
Hardback (1-87394-218-4)

Crucial Skills
An Anger Management and Problem Solving Teaching Programme for High School Students

Penny Johnson and Tina Rae

This 10 session programme helps students aged 11 to 16 deal with and manage their anger.

1999 • 98 pages
Paperback (1-87394-267-2)

www.luckyduck.co.uk

www.paulchapmanpublishing.co.uk

More On Anger Management

The Bubblegum Guy
How To Deal With How You Feel

Joost Drost *Consultant Clinical Psychologist, North Essex Mental Health Partnership Trust*

'These street-wise, cool kids enjoyed reading the story. They wanted to go straight through the story first (this surprised me). They wanted to keep the work and activities very private... they really seemed to need quiet reflection time'
- a teacher who used the materials with a group on anger management

Based on work done in a school in Essex, this is a heart-warming story that young people will associate with and reflect on. Bubble Gum Guy can't control his temper. When his feelings become too strong he covers all those around him with sticky yuck. This engaging story follows Guy on his journey of discovery to find ways of controlling his emotions. There are complete notes for school or home use and each part of the story is accompanied by a variety of interesting activities and worksheets.

The story, illustrations, worksheets and activities can be printed in colour from the accompanying CD-ROM. This book is suitable for class, small group or individual work with children aged nine to 13, and is also suitable for parents to use with their children.

This book helps young people to:

- learn to control their emotions
- express themselves in acceptable ways
- feel better about themselves
- lead happier lives

Contents

2005 • 115 pages
Paperback (1-904315-44-5)

www.luckyduck.co.uk

www.paulchapmanpublishing.co.uk PCP